The Basic Essentials of
ROCK CLIMBING

by Michael A. Strassman

**Illustrations by
John McMullen**

ICS BOOKS, Inc.
Merrillville, Indiana

THE BASIC ESSENTIALS OF ROCK CLIMBING

Copyright © 1989 by Michael A. Strassman

10 9 8 7 6 5 4 3 2 1

Printed in U.S.A.

Published by:
ICS Books, Inc.
One Tower Plaza
107 E. 89th Avenue
Merrillville, IN 46410

DEDICATION

This book is dedicated to my parents who showed me the beauty of wild places and to my climbing partner, Scott Ayers, whom I wish would slow down when running through talus.

ACKNOWLEDGEMENT

I would like to thank Doug Robinson, who helped give me my start and whose many words appear in this book and my editor Tom Todd, for giving me the chance to publish them.

PUBLISHER'S NOTE

Library of Congress Cataloging-in-Publication Data

Strassman, Michael A.
    Rock climbing : the basic essentials of / by Michael A. Strassman
  ; illustrations by John McMullen.
      p.   cm. -- (Basic essentials series)
    Includes index.
    ISBN 0-934802-45-9 : $4.95
    1. Rock climbing.   İ. Title.
GV200.2.S77   1989
796.5'223--dc20
                                    89-36057
                                    CIP

TABLE OF CONTENTS

Introduction iv
1. Fear and Other Misconceptions 1
2. Climbing Classifications 4
3. Equipment 9
4. Balance, Friction, and Movement 12
5. Footholds 18
6. Handholds 21
7. Opposition 28
8. Overhangs 32
9. Formations 36
10. Climbing Cracks 41
11. Safety 50
12. Practice 54
13. Why We Climb 57
       Appendix A 61

1. FEAR AND OTHER MISCONCEPTIONS

High on El Capitan in Yosemite Valley, two climbers struggle towards the rim. The leader has one foot twisted in a crack, the other foot frictions upon the face. A hand is securely wedged by a jammed fist, the other fiddles with a piece of protection. A rope runs down from the leader between many protection points to the belayer who is securely anchored to the wall. Beneath them, 2500 feet of space, twice the height of the tallest buildings on earth. The leader slips the protection in the crack, clips the rope through it and proceeds upward. One hand reaches higher and expands in the crack: a hand jam. The other hand steadies the body as the feet are moved. The foot comes up, slips in the crack sideways and twists. Once locked, the other hand moves in sequence. A rhythm develops. Foot, hand, foot, hand. Confidence exudes as the leader moves farther away from the last piece of protection.

In El Capitan Meadow, a busload of gawking tourists overruns the tall grass. They sport telephoto cameras and binoculars. Each wants to see "The Yosemite Climber". Being the height of summer, El Cap is littered with climbers. Six parties are ascending The Nose and several more are on The Shield. Perhaps twenty more parties can be found somewhere else on the huge expanse of granite. Someone shouts that they have seen the climbers. They point to long sinuous cracks about two-thirds of the way up. A small blue speck can be seen with a tinier speck climbing above it.

On the wall, the crack has gotten smaller. It is now the width of a finger. The leader inserts the hand to the knuckle and twists, a finger lock. The feet must come out of their secure placement in the crack and look for holds on the face. Awareness takes hold. The leader looks down for re-assurance. The belayer is casually watching a perigrine falcon circle lazily about the wall.

"Watch me", mutters the leader, "this is kinda thin."

The belayer looks up and tightens up the rope. The leader reaches higher and sinks another finger lock. The feet are rolled into a minuscule edge, trying to take advantage of the most friction. Another lock. Toes are pressed into the flaring crack.

Mind begins to take over, registering fears and admonitions. Adrenaline surges propelling strength ever upward. A large hold can be seen, just out of arms reach. A desperate lunge is needed. The leader clears all thoughts from the mind, concentrates on the hold and imagines catching it. The visualization is performed again. Commitment.

But thoughts of 2500 feet of exposure race in, along with doubts and the fear of failure. The leader yells down, "Watch MEEEEEEE!"

A foot leaves the rock and gravity takes hold. A fall. The last piece is not far; only four feet away. The belayer clinches the rope and the leader comes to a stop.

"Are you all right, Mary?" asks the belayer.

"No problem" she says, "just didn't have the psyc that time."

A cackling of voices erupts in the meadow. "A fall, A fall!", "Surely they have died.", "Can they be rescued?", "How do they get the rope up there?"

There are many misconceptions about rock climbing. Falls are rarely fatal. The climbers have brought the rope up there themselves, clipping it through pieces of protection as they go. If a fall should occur, they will only fall twice the distance to their last piece. The belayer stops the climber by stopping the rope. Falls are an important part of climbing. If we don't fall, we never push ourselves to our limits. We can only become better climbers by pushing ourselves and that's tough to do.

The biggest misconception about climbing is that climbers do not have fear. Everyone has an instinctive fear of heights and fear of falling. Climbing never removes those fears, it merely smooths them out. We know our bodies can accomplish the moves. It is the ever present void that restrains us, despite the rope and other precautions.

As we become better climbers, confidence begins to balance fear. You must be mentally secure in your abilities. Then you will be able to climb some amazing things.

The thought process Mary went through is typical of climbers. On easier ground, like the wide crack, we feel secure and confident. But as the climbing becomes more difficult our minds begin to work against us. Doubts are instilled and we loose our focus. In such situations it is best to relax. Clear the mind. Concentrate on the problem in front of you and commit yourself to achieving the movements. Visualize the move you are about to make and DO IT.

Sure, you are going to feel that adrenaline rush and fear will pervade your senses. Use it to your advantage. Channel that energy into making the move. Remember fear is healthy. It prevents us from making stupid mistakes. But being able to control that fearsome energy will make you a better climber.

2. CLIMBING CLASSIFICATIONS

There are many types of climbing. Climbing a monolith like El Capitan can be considered both rock climbing and mountaineering. Rock climbing is climbing on rock only, never snow and ice. If the weather should turn bad, Mary and her partner may have no choice but to practice mountaineering!

Rock climbing is further divided into free-climbing, artificial or aid climbing and free-soloing. Free-climbing is climbing without the use of technology to ascend the rock. Even though Mary had a rope on, it was not being used to get her up the cliff. It was used only as a safety device. Free climbing uses only your feet and hands.

The thin crack repelled a free climbing attempt. Now Mary will resort to aid or artificial climbing. Instead of climbing only with her feet and hands, she will place protection and stand on it. Here, security is dependent upon how well the protection is affixed to the rock, not the physical skills of the climber.

The difference is important. The goal of the climber is to climb as freely as possible. The purist's situation would be with no rope, bare feet and naked. This would not only be cold and hurt your toes, but would be very dangerous as well. But the concept remains the same. We climb using only our own bodies: ropes and hardware are only for safety.

Climbing high off the ground without ropes is not recommended. This is called "free-soloing". Though a highly respected art, free-soloing is like playing Russian roulette. A loose hold, rock-fall, or a sudden change in the weather could put an end to your climbing career and to you. Like the circus performer who works without a net free-soloer's are very confident of their ability. But even some very good climbers have met their maker while free-soloing.

Aid climbing should not be frowned upon. It has its merits. The majority of routes on a big wall like El Capitan can only be accomplished through aid climbing. Aid climbing can take you into some wild places. But since we are mostly concerning ourselves with the movement of rock climbing, we will not discuss aid climbing in this book.

Aid climbing is called SIXTH CLASS climbing. It is at the upper end of a rating scale for the difficulty of climbs. The reasoning being that if you could not free climb it, you may be able to aid climb it.

Rating Climbs

FIRST CLASS is the easiest. It can be compared to hiking up a steep hill.

SECOND CLASS climbing requires high steps, and rougher terrain.

THIRD CLASS begins to enter the realm of rock climbing. The hands must be used for balance and ascension. Third class is often called "scrambling".

FOURTH CLASS begins technical climbing. A fall is possible here. The climbing is still easy, but a fall could result in injury. You may want a rope on fourth class.

FIFTH CLASS climbing is very steep terrain where a fall will definitely result in death. A rope is absolutely necessary. The handholds are smaller than in fourth class climbing.

Fifth class has been subdivided into grades using a decimal system. At first, fifth class only went to 5.9. Climbers thought that anything harder than that would be Sixth Class climbing (aid climbing). But climbers excelled beyond 5.9. The hardest climbs in the world today are 5.14 and there will be harder climbs to come.

The rating of climbs is purely subjective. After someone has ascended a climb for the first time they give it a grade of difficulty based on the hardest move on the climb. Other climbers will climb the climb and confirm the grade. It may be adjusted up or down as a consensus is reached. There is no set definition for a certain grade of climbing. Climbs can even change their grade. Holds can break off making the climb easier or harder. As you become familiar with climbing grades you will know what a 5.8 feels like in comparison to a 5.10.

This system of rating just described is the American system of grading. There is a French system, an English system, an Australian system, etc. The American system is based on the hardest move on the climb. It doesn't take into consideration danger, severity or the quality of the climb.

Lately, in an attempt to compare it with other systems, a climb may be graded 5.14 even though it does not contain a single 5.14 move, but a string of 5.12 and 5.13 moves in a row. Hence, the continuousness of climbs begin to relate in the higher grades.

Leading a climb, as Mary was doing, is more difficult than following a climb. The leader can fall farther than the follower. The leader must also put in protection along the way. The follower has less risk and can relax more. Following climbs is good practice. Pulling out protection will help you to become a leader.

Even though leading feels more difficult, the grade remains the same. We are grading the difficulty of the moves, not how difficult it feels. Here is a loose description of the types of moves you will encounter on fifth class climbs:

5.0–5.5 Large holds evenly spaced. Like climbing a steep ladder.

5.6 The holds become smaller or oddly spaced. Cracks have secure jams.

5.7 The climbing requires certain techniques; the holds may be smaller; usually all four limbs are on the rock.

5.8 More technical. Holds may be smaller or involve sequential climbing. Cracks are steeper or jams may be oddly spaced.

5.9 The climbing requires more strength or the climbing is thinner. You may have only two limbs on the rock while reaching between moves.

5.10 The climbing may be overhanging with good holds, vertical with thin edges or low-angle with sequential movements and almost no holds. Cracks are smaller and sustained.

5.11 Overhanging with good edges, vertical with micro-edges, high-angled with no holds. Climbing is very sequential or sustained.

5.12 Overhanging with small edges, vertical climbing is very sustained, very sequential. May contain many 5.10 and 5.11 moves in a row.

5.13 Many 5.11 and 5.12 moves in a row with few or no rests. An example of a 5.13 move: With only the tips of your fingers in two small holes in the rock, lunge for a sloping hold on an overhanging wall, about four feet away. Now, put your feet on an edge the size of a toothpick and lunge for an even smaller hold. This is the crux sequence of the climb "Rude Boys" in Smith Rocks, Oregon.

5.14 Many 5.12 or 5.13 moves in a row. Sustained and sequential. Very rarely climbed in one try. As World Champion Stephan Glowacz said of America's hardest climb "To Bolt or Not To Be": "It is not so difficult climbing from bolt to bolt, but putting it together as one is really hard.". He attempted the climb for two weeks and could not climb it without a fall.

5.15 Hard.

The harder climbs, 5.11 and up, often take many attempts. This is known as gymnastic climbing. Like a gymnast, climbers will push themselves until they fall, trying to work out the sequence. Once a climb can be free climbed from the ground up without a fall, it is considered climbed. This is called a redpoint ascent.

If you can climb a climb without falling your first try; without ever having seen it before; or without watching anyone else on it, this is called an on-sight ascent.

If you have watched another person on a climb or have had the sequence of moves explained to you (the beta) and can do the climb without a fall first try, this is called a flash ascent.

Most beginners can climb a 5.6 climb first try without any problems. Intermediate climbers can climb up to 5.9. Advanced Intermediates can lead solid 5.10 and easy 5.11. Expert climbers can flash 5.12 and redpoint 5.13. There are very few climbers who can redpoint 5.14 and even fewer who can flash 5.14.

For now, you need not concern yourself with all these different types of climbing. You will be practicing free-climbing, pure and simple. Bouldering. All you need are your shoes, your muscles and your mind.

3. EQUIPMENT

Shoes

There is really very little equipment needed for climbing. Our muscles and tendons are our tools. The only piece of equipment we really need are shoes.

Shoes make climbing easier. The sole of the climbing boot is covered with a sticky rubber that adheres to the rock. A new pair of climbing shoes are so sticky that the soles will stick to themselves. The sticky rubber is a relatively new invention that has revolutionized climbing in recent years.

In the 1950's climbers used lugged soled mountain boots, akin to modern day hiking boots. Friction was obtained by the lugs clinging to grains in the rock. The boots were also very stiff, allowing the climber to stand on the tips of the toes.

In the mid 60's, flat soled climbing shoes became popular. Shaped like a high top tennis shoe, the shoes were lighter and had better rubber. Climbing standards rose as climbers donned such popular brands as P.A.'s, E.B.'s and R.R.'s (All named for the initials of the climbers that endorsed the shoes).

Throughout the 1970's the E.B. reigned supreme in the climbing world. Some of the hardest friction routes in Yosemite were climbed in these blue suede shoes. Then in the 1980's, the Fire' climbing boot burned all competitors. The boot had a sole of sticky Spanish rubber that changed the face of climbing. The shoes

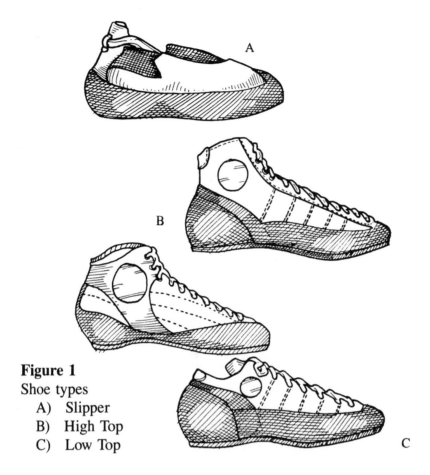

Figure 1
Shoe types
  A) Slipper
  B) High Top
  C) Low Top

would stick to anything, even a holdless rock wall. Climbers considered changing the grades of hard routes to easier grades, because the shoes were so good.

Today, shoes have become very specialized. There are shoes with sticky soft rubber for smooth faces; shoes with hard squared-off edges for micro-holds. Some shoes get their stiffness from a tight heel cup, a laced down high top or a carbon fiber insert. Many climbers own several pairs of shoes for different kinds of climbs.

The type of shoe you buy depends on many factors. A beginner should buy a friction shoe like the Fire' Classic. The stickyness will help you get around until your footwork becomes more proficient. As you get better, you can work into more specialized shoes.

They used to say that if the shoe doesn't hurt it's not tight enough. Don't believe it. Buy a shoe that's comfortable, yet snug. There is nothing worse than climbing all day with aching feet.

Chalk

Gymnastic chalk (Calcium Carbonate) has been one of the most noticeable changes in the history of climbing. Noticeable because it leaves white marks all over the rock. Sometimes it becomes so thick that the holds become slippery and the chalk must be cleaned off with a tooth brush. Chalk can also lead to holds breaking off as the calcium carbonate eats away at the rock.

Yet for all its negative attributes, chalk is a blessing. It serves the same purpose as it does for the gymnast: better grip by absorbing sweat and oils.

Chalk is carried in a chalk bag that is slung loosely around the waist. Before attempting a real difficult move you'll see a climber "chalk up". He or she will repeatedly dip into the bag and chalk again and again. This excessive chalking is usually caused by nervousness.

Chalk can be habit forming. It feels secure to have those fingers instantly dried. But the rock suffers because of it. If you use chalk, use it sparingly. When you are learning how to climb, don't use it at all. It isn't really necessary until you start climbing small hold face climbs.

Chalk starts to become a necessity on all climbs when it's hot. And that's too bad because desert areas that have less rainfall (to clean off the chalk) suffer. I suggest climbing in the shade during hot spells. It's more comfortable, your shoes stick better and you won't get sun burned.

That's it. Shoes and a chalk bag. All you really need to go climbing . . . except for two other items. Balance and friction.

4. BALANCE, FRICTION, MOVEMENT

Reduced to basic elements, climbing is dependent on balance and friction. Varying amounts of each keep us on the rock. Balance is where we place our weight, forward, backward, or to the side. Friction is how hard we press our shoes (or hands) onto the rock.

When we first get on the rock, we tend to want to hug the rock, we hold onto it for dear life. Your center of balance is off, so you grip harder. All of your weight is on your arms, making them tired. With no friction on the feet, they slide out from beneath you and . . . see ya!

After you've picked yourself out of the dirt, we'll show you the right way. Try and stand straight up and down. Find your center of balance and put your weight over the balls of your feet. Friction. Don't cling with your hands, use them only for balance.

Your legs are a lot stronger than your arms. When we climb, we want to use our legs as much as possible to take the strain off of our arms. When we begin to move, it is by moving the legs up, not the hands. Of course, on harder climbs you will have to rely on pulling up with the arms, but always look for a foothold to give those arms a break.

Remember, climbing shoes are bred for friction. They adhere so well that you do not have to press them into the rock. Step lightly and they stick. Climbing is not brute force overpowering

Figure 2
Proper balance; stand over
your feet when you can.

the stone, it's delicate, graceful movements. Good climbers seem
to move effortlessly, almost dance on the rock. Imitate these movements and you will become a better climber yourself.

Figure 3
Some footholds are
good to give your arms
a rest.

Movement

Climbing movements are similar to dance or gymnastics. They are fluid and precise. Graceful movements come from being relaxed. This may be tough to do your first time out on the rock.

When you begin to move, stay relaxed. Clear your mind of any negative thoughts or images. Don't think about falling or your mother in-law. Think about the problem in front of you. Make a mental picture of the move you are going to make. Visualize your body achieving the move. Now do it. Be committed. The slightest bit of hesitation and you won't make it.

When you move, move lightly, but with determination. Ease off one hold and place your foot directly onto the next. Do not drag or skip the foot up the rock. When you place the foot, don't put it someplace hoping to get a better purchase later. Put it where you need it. Now ease onto it, gently transferring your weight from one hold to the next. Let gravity do the work.

When you find a good hold, rest. Conserving energy is very important in climbing. Be direct. Exert only when you need to, and rest between exertions. A rest is a good time to relax the mind and body, consider the move in front of you, or just check out the view.

Climbing has been compared to chess, because of the planning involved. Look ahead and figure out your movements before you get there. The rock will dictate your movements; you must learn how to read it. Sometimes a move can only be accomplished through a certain sequence of movements. By planning ahead, you can execute that sequence and not become tired or unbalanced. Look ahead and let the rock tell you how to climb.

We don't always climb upward. Sometimes we must traverse, or even climb down. There are certain techniques for each direction of movement.

TRAVERSES

A traverse is any sideways movement. Traverses can be a lot of fun while bouldering. It's a good way to get pumped without getting too high off the ground. See how long you can hang on. You'll stay on a lot longer if you know some traversing techniques.

Hands are often crossed in a traverse. This allows you to reach

Figure 4
Proper balance

farther on the next move. But, don't get too crossed up, sometimes it is better to shuffle the hands from one hold to the other.

Feet can cross too. Again, don't get too crossed up. Always be looking ahead and planning your next move. Let the holds tell you how to climb.

Sometimes in a traverse there is only one hold for both hands.

In this case, you must match hands. Try to shift your hand to one side of the hold and grip it with your first two fingers. Then bring your other hand over and match the fingers onto the other side of the hold. Now remove the advancing hand and grab the next hold. Resteady all four fingers on the matched hold.

The same thing can be done with the feet. Place the foot to one side of the hold and bring the other foot onto the other side of the hold. Now remove the advancing foot and gain a better purchase with the other foot.

Sometimes you can match feet by hopping. Be sure that you have two good handholds and quickly replace one foot with the other. It'll amaze your friends.

DOWN CLIMBING

Climbing down is a lot harder than climbing up. It is more difficult to see the holds and to balance onto them once you've reached them. But down climbing is a skill every climber should know. It will get you out of some tricky situations. Climbers feel it is more honorable to downclimb than to fall. It's also a lot safer.

On really low-angle rock it is often best to climb down pointing outwards, with both hands and feet, (and occasionally your rear-end) on the rock. This is called a crab crawl. You can see your next holds, and a slip can be prevented simply by sitting down.

When it starts to get steeper, turn around. Look for your next holds by looking between your legs. If you must pull to one side or the other, use this opportunity to look down the unobstructed side. Always bring your feet down first and lower onto your arms. Once your feet are secure, place your hands on lower holds. If you are climbing down something you just climbed up, try and reverse the sequence exactly.

Always examine a downclimb before you attempt it. There is nothing more frightening than lowering towards a hold you cannot reach. Do not go past the point of no return hoping you will hit the hold. I did this once poised over a seventy-five foot chasm. I fell twenty feet and was saved by a wedged stone. Always be sure you are steadied on your foothold before removing your hands.

5. FOOTHOLDS

I cannot re-iterate this point enough; climb with the feet. Footwork is the key to good climbing. Knowing how to place your foot on a hold is of the utmost importance. There are many types of footholds and many ways to use them. Footholds can be as large as the rungs of a ladder or the thickness of a dime. You can stand on them all with proper footwork. For the most part, footholds can be classified into two groups, friction holds and edges.

The Edge

An edge is any squared-off hold that sticks out from the rock. Place the inside of your shoe, beneath the big toe, on the edge. Keep your ankles relaxed. Your shoe will provide the lateral stiffness.

As edges get smaller, not as much of your foot fits on the edge. Roll the foot into the edge, taking advantage of the most friction. Pressing the side or rand of the boot into the rock helps you stick.

As you become more experienced, you will learn to read the rock and know exactly which part of the shoe to use. Standing over the big toe is not the only way to stand on edge. On small steep edges, you may stand right on the point of the boot, perpendicular to the rock. Or perhaps the outside edge of the boot may be used to steady your balance to one side. Even the heel may be used. Footwork is a delicate art that takes years of practice. Be patient; you'll be surprised at the things you can do.

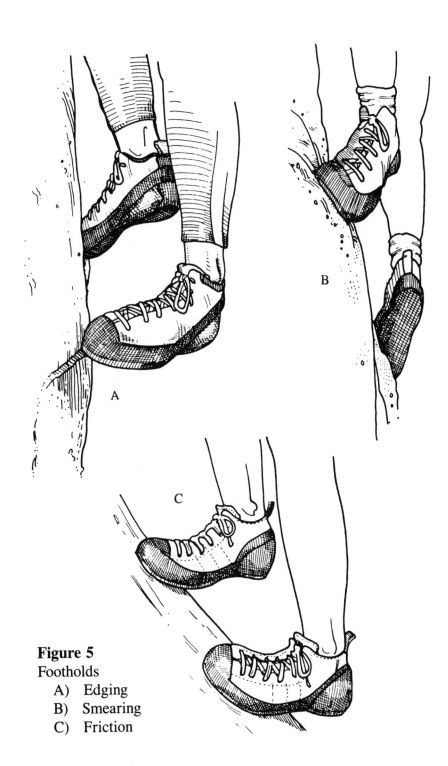

Figure 5
Footholds
    A)   Edging
    B)   Smearing
    C)   Friction

Friction Holds

Sometimes there is not an edge at all, but a small sloping protrusion. Or perhaps the rock isn't steep, maybe it has a low-angle and is glass smooth.

You must friction. Without an edge, friction climbing will seem scary at first. But actually it is easier than steep edge climbing. Look for the lowest angled portion of the rock and ease onto it. Press the entire ball of your foot on the hold and keep your heels high. On real thin holds, you may friction an edge, rolling the foot atop the edge. This is called smearing and can be done with either the inside or toe of the boot. Whichever way you place the foot, the important thing is to stay balanced over it.

When climbing on friction, it is best to keep moving. Often times your purchase is slippery at best; move through it quickly, but smoothly. Stop and rest when you have a good hold. Friction is the delicate side of climbing. Be aware, keep on your toes.

Friction climbing takes less strength than most other kinds of climbing. As a beginner, you will be able to climb moderate friction climbs with ease. These climbs are a good place to start out. Some of the best friction climbing in the world can be found in Tuolumne Meadows in the Sierra Nevada of California.

6. HANDHOLDS

When we begin to use the arms, they are mostly for balance. Our-weight should be on our feet. The arms act as a counterbalance as we move from side to side.

Positive Pulls

As the rock gets steeper, we need handholds. The best handholds are positive pulls, like the rungs of a ladder. As the holds get smaller, we must read the rock and learn how to use them.

There is no need for a white-knuckle death grip when grabbing hand holds. The art is in gripping just tight enough. The idea is to try and get as many fingers as you can on the hold. Even the thumb. It can wrap around the side of the hold or even hold the index finger down. This is called a ring grip.

Try to press the pads of your finger tips into the hold. Relax the fingers and open your hand into the rock. The palm may even conform to the rock, creating more friction. This is called the open grip.

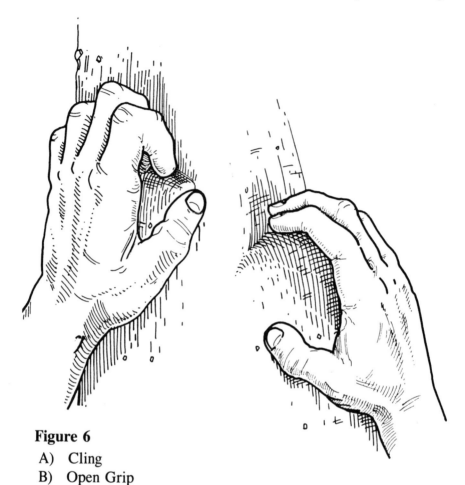

Figure 6
 A) Cling
 B) Open Grip

Work with the hold. Spread your fingers out until they find the best purchase. A little crystal may jut out, providing an in-cut to put a finger behind; or a small dish may swallow up a fingertip where there didn't seem to be a hold at all.

On smaller holds, you may try to arch the fingers inwards or outwards to try to press the pads into the hold (The cling grip and the vertical grip). Only use these grips when absolutely necessary. Over-use of these grips can cause serious tendon injury and arthritis.

Again, when not as many of your fingers fit, try and use the other fingers to help out. Often times you can stack one finger on top of another, especially in pockets.

Pinch Grip

Edges are not always straight-down positive pulls. Sometimes you may want to use the sides of the hold. If the hold has two sides, pinch it. The pinch grip can be really solid.

Side-Pulls

If there is only one side to a hold, it will work as well. It takes a little more balance, but side-pulls are very secure. You usually have to counter balance with the feet, pressing them into the rock as you pull on the side-pull hold. This is called opposition and is used alot in climbing.

A problem with side-pulls is the barn-door effect. You pull with the hands and push with the feet, and your body swings out into space. Try finding another side-pull or even a positive pull on the opposite side. Placing that opposite foot up high will also stop the barn door. The idea is to try and not pull so hard on the side-pull and distribute your force to the opposing side of the body.

Figure 7
Sidecling with barndoor.

Figure 8
Finger Pockets

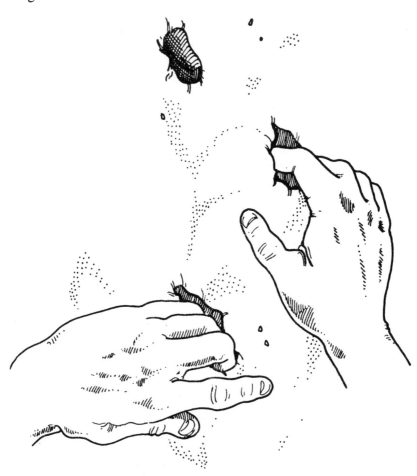

Pockets

Pockets, little holes in the rock, have become the new wave for extreme climbers. Formed by trapped gas or solutions in the rock, these little devils can be awfully fun to climb. The faces look like Swiss cheese, with an infinite variety of holds to choose from. Pocket climbing uses the same guidelines: get as many fingers as you can into the pocket.

You do not always pull straight down on a pocket. You can use the side or even the top of the pocket. The variations are endless.

Figure 9
Pinch Grip

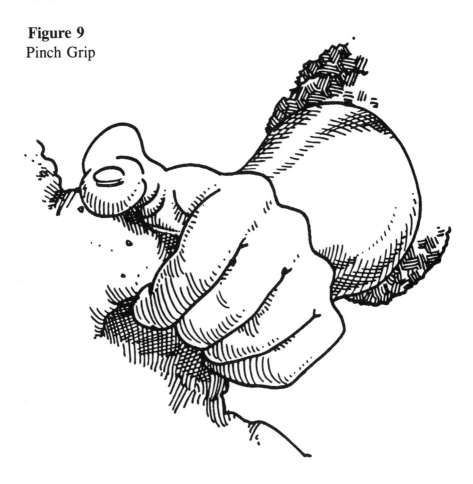

Palming and Push-Offs

Sometimes the holds are rounded or sloping. These holds must be palmed. Place your entire hand flat on the hold and press it into the rock. Don't let go once you've pulled up; push off in the opposite direction. Push-offs really help keep you in balance. Opposition again. Your advancing hand is pulling and the palming hand is pushing.

If there is only one hold, or a flat ledge, you may have to mantle. A mantle is similar to boosting yourself on top of a wall. Grab the ledge, work your feet up and push-off with both hands. Lock the elbows. Now, step the feet up high until they are on the ledge. (Don't use your knees. This is considered bad form.) Now, stand-up. Look for a higher hold to steady yourself.

Figure 10
Mantle

Remember, use the feet. Use them to push you towards higher hand holds. If you come to a spot where there are no footholds, friction the feet on the vertical rock and reach. They'll stick! If you absolutely cannot reach a hold, you may have to lunge for it.

Lunges

Lunging is an art in itself. Here you cross the line between static climbing and dynamic climbing. Static climbing is reaching from one hold to another always in control. Dynamic climbing involves spurts of energy to reach holds. Monkeys swing from tree to tree dynamically, but they climb up the trunk of the tree statically.

Lunges take a lot of practice. Bend the knees, look at the hold, focus on it, and picture in your mind jumping up and grabbing the hold. No doubts. Be committed. DO IT!

Lunges seem impossible sometimes. But a positive mental attitude will produce some astonishing results. One of the great masters of lunges is John Gill. This man would lunge for a hold, push-off of it, and lunge for the next hold in one smooth motion. It's beautiful and graceful to watch, you'll be lucky if you can lunge as well as John Gill.

7. OPPOSITION

Sometimes, none of our handholds are positive pulls. They point downward or are tilted to the side. Opposing forces will keep us on the rock. Opposition is pushing or pulling in opposite directions. It works so well, you can climb overhangs using it.

Stems

The most classic opposition is the stem. It is used for climbing between two planes of rock, like in a chimney or a corner. You press your feet against either wall and bridge upwards. Press the hands (or pull with the hands) and move the feet. As the walls become farther apart, you must really stretch, as if doing the splits. This takes some flexibility.

Stems are not limited to fissures and chimneys. They can be done between two sideways holds. They are often good enough to give your arms a rest.

Knee-Back

As the fissure gets smaller, you can oppose your knee and your hands against your foot and your back. Press your foot and your knee against one wall and raise your torso. Now press your hands and your back against the other wall and move the legs up. It is slow going, but very effective. Knee pads are recommended.

Figure 11
Chimney climbing; knee up

Figure 12
Layback

Layback

A layback is used in conjunction with the side-pull. You pull with your hands and push with your feet. The classic lay-back occurs in a corner with a crack. Grab the side of the crack high with the hands, sit back and push with the feet. Now move a hand, then a foot, now a hand, then a foot. A rhythm develops. Keep going. If you stop and rest on one arm, you'll get tired quickly. In steep laybacks, it helps to have your feet up high.

Figure 13
Undercling

Undercling

When all the holds point down, you must undercling. Underclings are often done on downward pointing flakes. Pull outward on the flake and push with the feet. Be sure that the flake is well attached, for underclings exert a lot of stress. Knock on it. If it vibrates or sounds hollow, pick another route.

Combinations

I have described the classic forms of these movements. Often times you must use a combination of these holds. A layback is an excellent way to reach higher handholds. A stem will often turn into a layback by reaching towards a side-pull. An undercling may be used to get you through an overhang. As you get to know the rock better, you'll be able to see exactly which sequence to use. Climbing will become intuitive. Let those primal instincts come alive!

8. OVERHANGS

Overhangs are intimidating. It seems impossible that humans can climb a rock upside-down. But if the holds are large, overhangs can be easy to master.

Of course, overhangs take a lot more strength than low-angle climbs. The secret to climbing them is conserving that strength. Hang with the arms straight, and keep the feet tucked into the rock. Move efficiently through overhangs; calmly, rhythmically and deliberately.

Heel Hooks and Toe Locks

Always keep those feet pressed underneath you. Don't let your legs swing out. Sometimes you can throw a heel hook up high. Camming your toes against your heel is even more secure. A toe lock.

Visualizing the sequence through the overhang helps you move smoothly. If you must rest, hang with arms straight. But don't hang out for a long time. Keep moving.

Figure 14
Heel hook

Figure 15
On overhangs, keep your
arms straight as you move
your feet up.

The Deadpoint

The most efficient way to move through overhangs is a technique called deadpointing. Simultaneously, pull-in with your arms, push-off with your feet and reach for the next hold. This technique was developed by basketball players to get the maximum height out of their jump shot. You want to be grabbing the next hold at your maximum height and extension. The moment before gravity takes effect is called the deadpoint.

The Lip

Often, overhangs will have a large hold at the end of the overhang, the lip. Use this to turn the overhang. As you come around it, try and keep your weight out from the rock. Don't stay tucked in. Keep your body stretched out.

Once you're standing on the lip, look down between your legs. There is nothing between you and the ground. It's a great feeling.

And don't think that overhangs are always difficult. One of the most classic overhangs is a 10 foot roof called "The Geronimo" in Joshua Tree. A crack splits the overhang clear to the summit block. You can reach through to grab big holds inside. A Thankgod hold greets you at the lip. The climb is rated 5.7.

There is an overhang on an Austrialian sea cliff called "Fear." It overhangs 50 feet, in 150 feet of climbing. Giant shelfs and Thank-god holds take you out over the ocean to the lip. It is rated 5.7.

9. FORMATIONS

In order to read the rock, you must have a vocabulary to work with. There are many different types of formations. Some are unique to certain types of rocks, others can be found in all kinds of rock.

Large Formations

Mountains have ridges that radiate from the summit. When these are sheer and knife-edged, they are called aretes. Often a ridge will end abruptly in a large rock face. This is called a buttress. Pinnacles or spires are thin shafts of rock that stick out from the surrounding terrain. Pinnacles are not always solitary monuments. A shaft of rock than leans against a cliff may be called a pinnacle. If you like climbing spires, Pinnacles Nat'l Monument in South Dakota has some beautiful pinnacles.

Climbing is not always found in the mountains. An outcrop or a small dome may suffice. A dome is a formation that is steep at the bottom and gradually loses its steepness towards the top. Domes are often found in granitic rocks and are formed through a process called exfoliation. Exfoliation is the cracking and peeling of successive layers like the skin of an onion. The rounded side of Half Dome in Yosemite Valley is a classic example of exfoliation.

Figure 16
Rock formations

Dihedrals

When a vertical crack interrupts an exfoliation layer, a corner may be formed. This is called a dihedral or open book. A dihedral is any meeting of two planes of rock. Dihedrals can be fun to climb. Stems, laybacks and classic crack climbing can be found in dihedrals. "The Good Book" in Yosemite Valley is an excellent dihedral climb.

Flakes

A flake is where two layers meet, usually at an acute angle. Flakes can be underclinged or laybacked, but be careful. The edges of flakes are sometimes rotten or the flake may be detached. A falling detached flake can sever a rope.

Outside Corners

An outside corner has come to be known as an arete. No one thought of climbing these aretes until recently. Good holds, opposition and pinches can be found on aretes. "The Latest Rage" in Smith Rocks, Oregon and "The Millstone Edge" in England are good examples of arete climbs.

Cracks

A crack that is not in a dihedral is called a straight-in crack. Cracks vary in size from seams to chimneys. They are classified by the techniques used to climb them. Seams are so small you can't get your fingers in them; tips take only your finger tips; next is finger cracks, off-fingers, hand cracks, off-hands, fist cracks, off-widths, squeeze chimneys, and chimneys. The best crack climbing in the U.S. is found outside of Canyonlands Nat'l Park in Utah.

Overhangs

Climbs are classified by their angle of steepness. Slabs or aprons are low angle climbs. Near-vertical are called faces. Past vertical is called overhanging. Overhangs are further classified into bulges, roofs (or ceilings) and headwalls. A bulge is a portion of rock that overhangs, becomes vertical, then lessens in steepness. A roof is an overhang that just out horizontally from the rock. A headwall is a large expanse of overhanging rock. The Shawangunks of New York have a great concentration of overhangs.

Small Formations

Erosion has created formations on a smaller scale. A pocket is a hole in the rock. A hueco is a large depression in the rock. When the rock is granular and disintegrating the depression is known as a bowl. Most huecos are polished with varnish. Hueco Tanks, a climbing area in Texas, is where the name came from.

Figure 17

Features of Rock

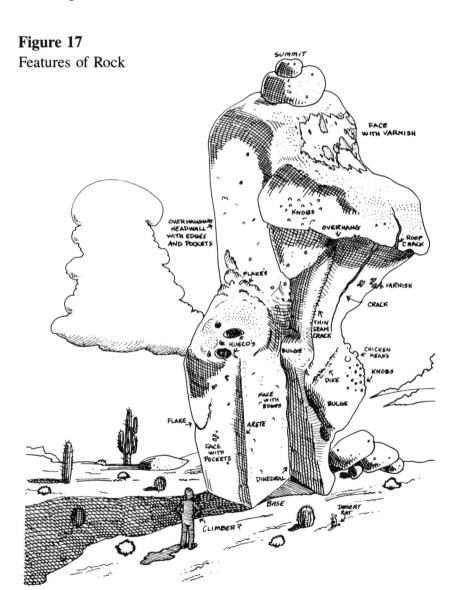

Case-Hardening

Varnish or patina is a super hardened surface of the rock that often forms edges. Also called case-hardening, this weathering phenomenon occurs when water trapped inside the rock dissolves minerals and brings them to the surface. Behind every piece of varnish is a zone of disintegrated rock. If the case hardening is thick enough, the edges will support more than body weight. But be careful. Check out varnished edges before using them. The Red Rocks of Nevada outside of Las Vegas has many varnished cliff faces.

Chickenheads

When varnish is eroded, a horn or chickenhead will form. A chickenhead resembles its namesake: a bulbous protrusion with a thin neck. If the neck of the chickenhead is varnished then these formations can be trusted. If it looks granular and rotten, don't trust it. Huge faces of chickenheads can be found in the Cochise Stronghold of Southern Arizona.

Intrusions

Intrusions are any type of rock that forms inside another rock while it was beneath the earth. A dike is a sinuous rib of harder rock that has eroded out from the surrounding rock. Dikes can be pinched or traversed. "Pinched Rib" in Joshua Tree Nat'l Monument is a short but classic dike.

Knobs

A knob is a large crystal that sticks out. Knobs can be edged, grasped or pinched. They are usually composed of crystals of a single mineral. Knobs are also found in sedimentary rocks. Tuoulmne Meadows in the Sierra Nevada has many knobby faces.

Polish

Polish is different from case-hardening in its formation. Polish is formed in two ways. Water may polish the rock or glaciers may create it. It tends to be slippery, even for today's miracle boots. The polish formed by glaciers will chip-off to form amazing edges.

These are most of the formations you will encounter. Local areas have their own names. A couple I've heard are pebbles, bricks, erratics, nipples, bananas, etc. A good imagination is needed when naming these formations. Have fun with it.

10. CLIMBING CRACKS

The majority of rock climbs follow a weakness in the rock. A crack. Crack climbing is not natural like face climbing. It involves specialized movements depending on the size of the crack. It is an acquired skill that takes lots of practice.

Cracks are climbed by a technique called jamming. You expand a part of the body that fits in the crack. This could be a finger or your entire torso. It is best to look for a constriction in the crack, although all jams can be performed in parallel-sided cracks.

Hand Cracks

The hand crack has the most secure jams. The entire hand slides into the crack and the thumb rolls into the palm. The hand expands and locks in place. The feet are slipped in sideways and twisted into the crack. Sometimes the foot jams are so good they are hard to remove. Lowering down slightly will often get them unstuck.

Move rhythmically. Place a high jam, then a lower jam to steady yourself. Move a foot up, then advance with the lower jam. Move the feet. Move a hand. Foot. Hand. Foot. Hand.

High jams are placed thumbs up for maximum reach. Lower jams or jams in diagonaling cracks are placed thumbs down. Thumbs down is made more secure by bringing your elbow down. This helps cam the hand.

Thin Cracks

Thin cracks are harder to climb than hand cracks. They are most difficult when you cannot get a finger in the crack. Any edge or opening must be utilized. Often times you must layback the crack with your fingertips. Desperate.

Figure 18
Small fingerlock

Figure 19
Small fingerlock

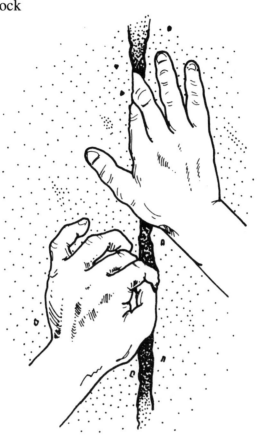

Finger Jams

When it begins to open up, you may only be able to get one or two fingers in. Sink the fingers to the knuckle (if you can) and stack one finger on top of the other. Now twist the fingers. This is called a finger lock. Again, thumbs down is more secure.

Feet are harder to get into a thin crack. Press the tip of the boot into the crack. This is called toeing in. If your boot is thin enough, try twisting the tip of the boot into the crack. This is called a toe jam.

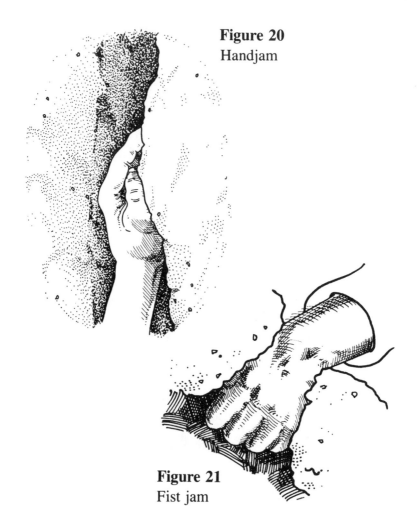

Figure 20
Handjam

Figure 21
Fist jam

Off-hands and Fist Jams

As the crack gets wider we must expand the hand jam. The off-hands or rattly hand ham is accomplished by cupping the hand and camming the knuckles against the fingers and the wrist. Wider, you turn the jam horizontally and make a fist. The fist jam.

Off-Fingers

Off-fingers jams are where you can get your knuckles in the crack but not your entire hand. These jams are difficult to secure. The thumb is placed below the fingers inside the crack and the arm rotates downward to cam the jam in place. The off-finger jam is one of the most difficult jams to master.

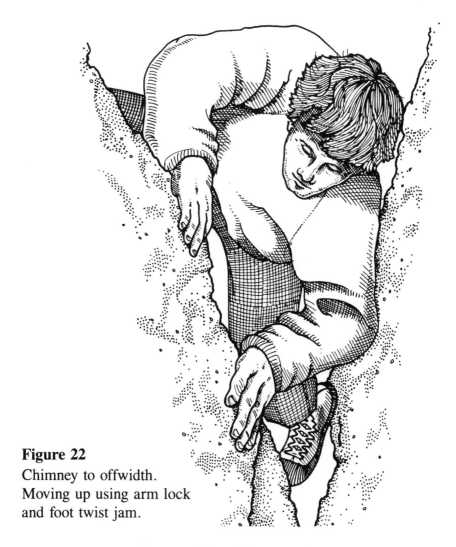

Figure 22
Chimney to offwidth.
Moving up using arm lock
and foot twist jam.

Off-Widths

Any larger than the fist jam, and things really get disgusting. The dreaded off-width. Classic off-width technique is slow going. Fit as much of your body as you can into the crack. Your toe presses against one wall and your heel ratchets down against the other wall to lock the foot in place. The arm can go in two ways: extended, for smaller off-widths or compressed for slightly larger ones. Either way the palm is cammed against the elbow and shoulder. Move up by using the heel-toe to get you higher and replacing the arm each time.

Figure 23
Offwidth arm lock.

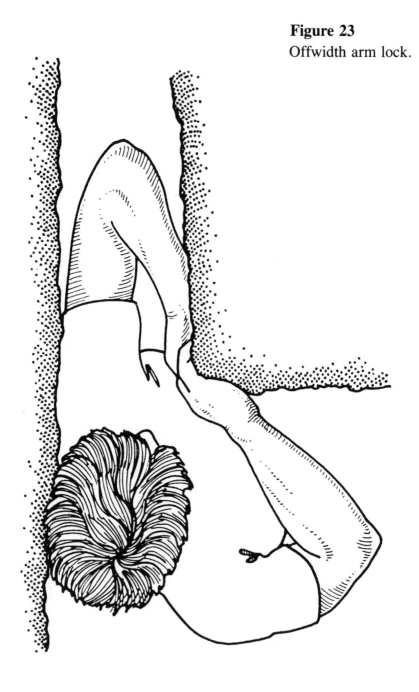

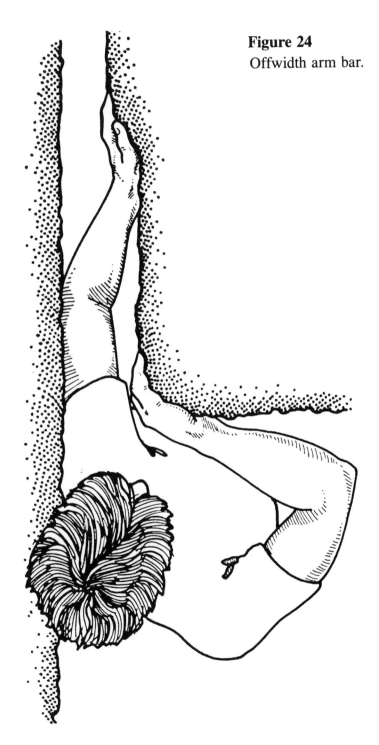

Figure 24
Offwidth arm bar.

Figure 25
Offwidth; one type of hand
stack.

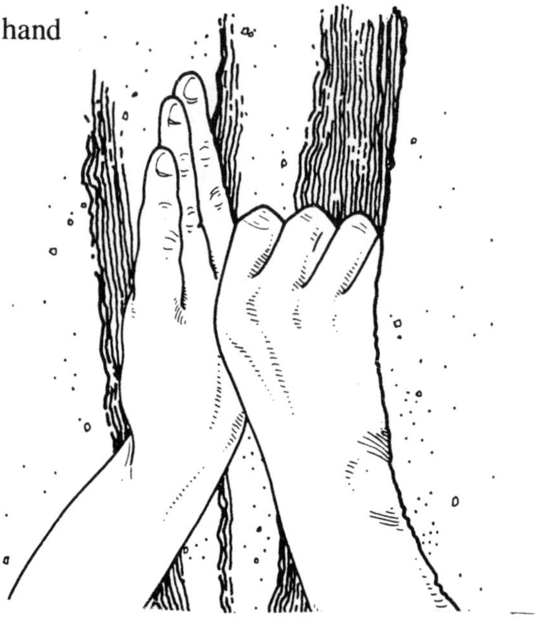

Leavittation

A different way to climb off-widths was discovered by a fellow
named Randy Leavitt. Called Leavittation, this technique utilizes
handstacks, knee locks and heel jams. It is very difficult to master.
The handstack is created by placing the palm flat against one wall
and wedging the fist against the other wall between the back of the
hand. Now, lock the knee (camming between legs and knee) as
high as possible underneath the handstack. Cam your toe and heels
against the outside of the crack. Once the knee lock feels secure,
let go of your hands and place a higher handstack. This is the most
difficult part. Try to palm and layback one side of the crack until
you are centered over the knee lock.

You have to choose a side when Leavittating, for you will
always place the same knee. The hand with which you wedge your
fist will be the same side as the knee lock.

There are many different ways of Leavittating. Instead of a
knee lock, you may place a heel jam above your head. Your handstack may consist of two hands wedged back to back. Climbers
have even wedged a hand against the side of their head. A head
jam!

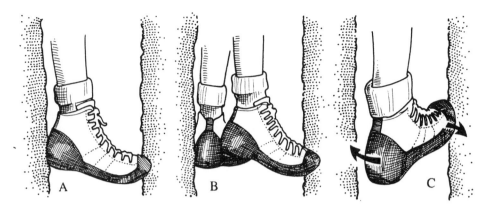

Figure 26

A) Offwidth Heel to Toe
B) Offwidth T-Foot Stack
C) Offwidth Twist Jam

Crack and Face Combinations

Whenever possible, look for other holds. Sometimes you may jam the hands and stem with the feet. Or layback off of a jam. A foothold may provide better purchase than toeing in. Keep your eyes open for all the possibilities.

Taping Up

Climbers will often protect their hands with adhesive cloth tape. It is advisable for beginning crack climbers to tape up. The inexperienced tend to thrash the jams into the crack, creating small cuts knows as gobis. Once you've got a gobi, you might as well say good-by to crack climbing until they are healed. Learn to place the jam smoothly. It helps save energy—and skin.

In real rough rock, taping up is mandatory. There are many ways to tape. Find a method that suits you the best. You want to cover the knuckles, the back of the hand, and the wrist. Don't tape too tightly. It will decrease your range of motion and constrict your blood vessels.

One of the ugliest things to see at popular climbing areas is little pieces of tape lying about the ground. Never leave tape or any trash at the base of climbs. Pack it out, even if it is not your own.

Once you have mastered crack climbing, you'll be hooked. As the great Sierra mountaineer Doug Robinson says, "Cracks are the boldest features on the rock, but climbing them is subtle . . . they are a privilege to climb."

11. SAFETY

Climbing has earned a reputation as a dangerous sport. The label is well-earned. Climbing is often practiced in dangerous terrain, far from medical help. Hence, it is good to know what can be done to make it safer. If you take the proper precautions, climbing can be safer than driving a car.

Be Aware

Most climbing injuries occur while approaching or leaving the climb. Descents are especially treacherous. Our awareness is sharpened while on the climb, but we tend to get lackadaisical once on the descent. Serious downclimbing may be encountered or we may find ourselves poised over a big drop. Straighten up and pay attention! Don't kick back until you're safely home in bed.

I have a friend who is always in a hurry. An accomplished mountaineer, his speed has saved him from spending a night out without a sleeping bag. Although speed is important, you have to keep your eyes open. This fellow loves to run through talus: leaping and jumping from boulder to boulder. But one twisted ankle and he's spending the night. Boulder hopping also puts extreme pressures on the knees. Pick your way carefully through the talus. Try to downclimb instead of leaping.

Bouldering Safety

We must fall if we want to push ourselves, but we do not want to get injured. Have a spotter underneath you. He isn't there to catch you, just to break your fall, to lessen the impact. Try not to boulder over rocky places. Also, be sure to move brush and rocks away from the landing zone. Try to downclimb if you can't do the problem. It will save your knees and it's a good way to practice your downclimbing skills.

Those downclimbing skills may not help you if you break the first two rules of bouldering, "Don't climb too high" and "Never climb up anything you can't climb down". Height is relative. You can hurt yourself falling from any height. That's why it is good to remember the third rule "Never climb alone".

Stretching and Conditioning

Climbing movements are not typical of everyday actions. You will find yourself bending in places you never thought possible, executing the splits, and torquing on your arms. Stretching and conditioning are of prime importance to prevent injury.

You have to be physically fit to rock climb. If your muscles and tendons are not prepared for the stresses you will put upon them, you may hurt yourself. Work out with many repetitions of light weights to build your muscles up. Keep up your cardiovascular fitness to provide endurance. Don't over do it though. Doing pull-ups with weights around your waist is not recommended. Find a physical trainer to help you out.

You don't have to be a muscle-bound meathead to rock climb; on the contrary, strength to weight ratio is very important. You want to be lean and have good muscle tone.

Once you've built up a little strength, bouldering is a perfect way to stay in climbing shape. Always stretch before you get on the rock. Standing on the ground, grab a handhold and stretch off of it. Shoulders, arms, back, torso and legs. Stretch those tendons and ligaments. They will be more supple and harder to injure.

Tendonitis

The most common climber injury is chronic tendonitis. It comes from over using a particular tendon. The first signs of tendonitis is inflammation in the joint area. Lay-off immediately. Once the pain subsides, don't go climbing. Start working out the joint with very light weights until you feel no pain for about two weeks. Icing the joint and taking an anti-inflammatory like ibuprofen helps. Consult your doctor. He or she is the best one to advise you on the proper therapy.

Tendonitis commonly occurs in the shoulders, elbows and fingers. Taping the fingers between the joints helps support those tendons. Building up the muscles is the only way to prevent other forms of tendonitis. Try to avoid climbs that inflame a certain joint. Pocket pulls can hurt the fingers; thin face climbing gets the elbows; laybacks can hurt the shoulders.

Abrasion and Impact

The other most common injury is abrasion and impact. It is recommended that you wear knee-pads, elbow pads and a helmet when you climb. But this is cumbersome and impractical. If you are skillful, you will not bump your head. I wear a helmet if there is a danger of falling rock. I never wear elbow pads. I always wear knee pads. An impact to the knee can damage the knee permanently. Besides, it is a lot more comfortable in squeeze chimneys and off-widths.

Abrasion is a fact of life in climbing. Thrash around in any fist crack and you're bound to draw some blood. Taping up to the elbow is impractical. Careful climbing is the cure. Be precise when placing jams or moving over the rock.

On rough rock, your fingertips may become soft and tender. Try to break them in slowly. Climb until you feel them sting, then quit. Keep doing this until you've built up some calluses. If you keep climbing on tender tips you will get a divit in the finger. These take a long time to heal. Lifting weights and playing guitar helps build finger tip calluses.

Objective Dangers

An objective danger is any risk you cannot control. Objective dangers like weather and loose rock do their share of killing. Yet, awareness will lessen the chances. If the weather is looking ugly, get out. Have the proper clothing, extra food and water. Never climb in a lightning storm. You are a natural lightning rod standing atop a boulder. Be aware of loose rock. If the stone sounds hollow or vibrates when you tap it, stay away. Examine flakes and holds carefully. Make sure they are attached somewhere to the cliff.

First Aid

Always have a first aid kit handy and some working knowledge of first-aid. Your kit should contain band-aids, bandages, gauze, ace bandage, scissors, tweezers, a small bottle of hydrogen-peroxide and aspirin[1]. If you've neglected to bring one, athletic tape and water can do wonders. But know how to use it. A course in Advanced First Aid is recommended for any outdoor sports enthusiast.

The best prevention against injury is awareness. Know your limits, know how strong and supple you are, know a little about first-aid. Be prepared. Climbing safety systems are not foolproof. You can die climbing. But death and injury can be avoided through proper prevention and awareness.

[1]Further discussion of medical care can be found in *Wilderness Medicine*, by William Forgey, M.D., ICS Books, Inc., 107 E. 89th Ave., Merrillville, IN 46410

12. PRACTICE

Now that you know a little technique you'll want to try it out. Be careful. Don't rush off with a bundle of clothesline and a pair of tennis shoes. Find some more experienced climbers to introduce you to the sport.

Many communities have climbing clubs, outdoor recreation programs or search and rescue organizations that can lead you to other climbers. Perhaps your best source is your local outdoor sports shop. They can show you the proper equipment, latest techniques and put you in touch with a guide.

Find A Guide

Learning how to climb from a guide is the best way to learn. He'll rope you up safely and show you the proper techniques for setting up a top rope. Top roping exceeds bouldering for practice. You climb higher, pushing your strength and endurance. A fall is very comfortable. The rope stretches a little and you come to a soft stop.

When seeking a guide, be sure that they are certified by the American Mountain Guides Association. There are many irreputable guides out there operating without permits and insurance. Look for the A.M.G.A. logo. The A.M.G.A. is the only guide certification body in the U.S. To locate a certified Mountain Guide write:

The American Mountain Guides Association
P.O. Box 699
Leavenwoth, WA. 89926

Climb With Better Climbers
Once you've become a little more proficient, try to find some better climbers to climb with. Follow climbs at your limit or a little harder. Push yourself. Take falls. This is the only way you will become better. Ask questions of the better climbers. Get to know your body, its strengths and weaknesses. Keep climbing.

Boulder
Boulder whenever you can. If the weather is foul or the rocks are too far away, you may want to build an artificial climbing gym. You can purchase pre-made holds that bolt on to plywood or a wall. Mix them around to create a variety of sequences. Overhang the plywood a little to make it harder.

Climbing Gyms
In some large cities there are climbing gyms. These are huge indoor walls of artificial climbing holds, rope ladders and peg boards. Trainers at climbing gyms can tailor a work out to your physique and climbing ability. They are knowledgeable about climbing injuries and know how to prevent them. Climbing gyms are a wonderful source of information.

Imaging
Watching climbing helps too. While resting at the crag or at the gym, watch others climb. Try to execute their moves in your head. This is called imaging. Conscious visualization of climbing movements will help your own climbing.

There are even "rock" videos. *Moving Over Stone*[2] is a video that uses the process of imaging. The tape is designed to be watched over and over. Every type of move is depicted by some of the best climbers in the world. It is an exciting and entertaining video to watch. It actually sharpens climbing skills.

But don't sit around watching TV. Get out there and DO IT. The only way to get better is to push yourself and climb a lot. Practice makes perfect.

[2]*Moving Over Stone* is available from your favorite climbing equipment shop, ICS Books, Inc., or from Range of Lights Productions, P.O. Box 2906, Mammoth Lakes, CA 93546 for only $39.95.

13. WHY WE CLIMB

The sun departs the western sky. On El Capitan, a hand reaches over the rim searching for a handhold. A varnished chickenhead reflects the setting sun, then is covered by the hand. Mary works her feet up and mantles. She is on top. Barely able to contain her excitement, she rests a moment, then sets up the belay.

One hundred fifty feet below, her partner awaits the signal that the climb is finished. Beneath them, the ground has steadily dwindled away for the last five days, yet the view has never been boring. Up valley she can see the alpenglow spread over the face of Half Dome. Down valley, the cities of the Great Central Valley are turning on their lights. Elsewhere, people are stuck in traffic jams or anticipating the dinner rush. Here there is calm . . . and beauty.

"OFF-BELAY!", comes the call. The big wall climb of a lifetime has come to an end. Jessica pulls herself over the rim in the fading light and the two partners hug each other in congratulations.

As if signalled by the ringmaster of the gods, the skies ignite in hues of crimson and vermillion. A far away lightning storm adds to the display. A snowy owl swoops from his perch and begins the night foray. Mary turns to her partner and says softly, "This is why I climb."

As two Englishmen, Mallory and Irvine, set off for Mt. Everest, a reporter asked them the inevitable question, "Why do you climb?". The chaps reply has become cliche, "Because it's there!" they said.

As for myself, I don't like that answer. I think every climber has his or her own personal reasons, each distinct and individual from the next. Some people like the physical challenge, others like the problem solving involved. Like Mary and Jessica, everyone enjoys being in the natural element, amongst the cliffs, the lichens and the steel blue skies.

The response, "Because it's there!", brings up connotations of man's supremacy over nature. Just because it is the tallest or the steepest, it must be conquered and trampled upon. Climbing is an unusual sport, it is easy to become egotistical about our achievements. But remember, we are treading in nature's garden, we must be careful how we step. Nature should be respected, not conquered.

Unfortunately, the crags have suffered from the assault of the ego. Holds are chiseled to make an impossible route climbable; offensive bolts are chopped leaving ugly scars in the rock; and routes are squeezed in already crowded faces, so a climber can get his name in a guidebook. These acts detract from the climbing experience. Climb for yourself, not to make a statement. If you ruin the rock resource, you ruin it for everyone.

Competition is inevitable in rock climbing. Unlike tennis or bicycle racing, there are no clear cut winners. Only a rating scale to judge your success. Comparisons will be made, especially as you become more skilled. Do not heed it, climb for fun. The place for competition is at the bouldering contest or on the artificial rock wall, not on the crags.

We climb for enjoyment, pure and simple. It doesn't matter how we got up the rock or who is better than who, what matters is that you have fun. Competition is alright, as long as the rock doesn't suffer in the process.

Ego aside, the rock suffers due to neglect. Our vertical playground is a recreational resource that will be used by many people for years to come. Already crags in places like Joshua Tree and Yosemite are beginning to feel the effects of over-population. Litter lines the cliffs, trails criss-cross through the brush, and the rock itself is littered with chalk, slings and expansion bolts.

Treat the rock as if it were your mother. Mother Earth. Follow established paths, pick up litter and leave little trace of your passing. The reason why we climb will become self-evident. To be out there, to become part of it, to do it.

So what are you waiting for? Have fun. Go climbing!

APPENDIX A

GLOSSARY

Aid Climbing: Using artificial aids to ascend the rock.

Anchor: Main protection point in a roped safety system.

Apron: A low-angle slab of rock.

Arete: 1) A sheer knife-edged ridge. 2) An outside corner.

Balance: Where we place our center of gravity.

Barndoor: The tendency of the body to swing out from the rock when executing a layback or using a sidepull.

Belay, Belayer: In a roped safety system, the belay is the point where the rope is fed out, taken in, or stopped to catch falls. The belayer is one who does this.

Beta: An explanation of the sequence of climbing movements for a particular climb.

Bouldering: Climbing without ropes close to the ground.

Bucket: An in-cut hand hold.

Bulge: A portion of the rock that becomes overhanging then lessens in steepness.

Buttress: A large face that protrudes from a ridge or slope.

Cam: A twisting motion that uses opposing forces to hold a part of the body in place.

Case-harding: Mineralization of the surface of the rock that produces holds. Also called Patina or Varnish.

Chalk: A substance used to dry sweat and oils from the hands.

Chickenhead: A protruding erosion feature characterized by a thin neck where it is attached to the rock.

Chimney: A large crack in the rock that is big enough to fit your entire body. A Squeeze Chimney fits only a part of your body.

Ceiling: An overhang that juts out horizontally from the rock.

Cling Grip: Arching the fingers inward on a handhold.

Corner: The meeting point of two planes of rock. Also called a Dihedral or Open Book.

Crab Crawl: Facing outward while descending.

Cross-hands, Cross-feet, cross-over, cross through: The act of
  crossing feet or hands to accomplish further reach on the next
  move.

Deadpoint: The point of maximum extension while lunging.

Dihedral: See Corner.

Dike: A vein of harder rock that protrudes from the surface.

Dome: A large rock that lessens in steepness towards the top.

Dynamic Climbing: Jumping or lunging movements.

Edge, Edging, Edging Boot: A squared off hand or foothold;
  Pressing the edge and side of the boot into the hold; A boot
  with stiff soles and harder rubber.

Exfoliation: The erosion of successive layers of rock.

Exposure: Increased height and steepness.

Finger Crack, Finger Lock: A thin crack that fits only your fingers; twisting of the fingers in a finger crack.

Fifth Class Climbing: Near vertical climbing where a fall would
  result in death.

First Class Climbing: Walking up a steep hill.

Fist crack, Fist jam: A crack whose width is the same as your
  fist; expanding your fist in a jam.

Flake: Where two layers of rock meet.

Flash Ascent: Completing a climb for the first time without
  a fall.

Follower: The second person in a roped climbing party that removes the protection.

Fourth Class Climbing: Climbing on large holds on steep rock.
  A fall may result in injury or death.

Free climbing: Climbing using only your hands and feet. A rope
  may be used for safety, but not for ascension.

Free soloing: Climbing without ropes where a fall could kill you.

Friction: How hard you press into the rock.

Friction Hold, Friction Boot: A hold that is not positive, but
  lower angled or sloping; A boot with a soft rubber soul.

Hand Crack, Hand Jam: A crack that is the width of your hand;
  rolling the thumb into the palm to create a jam.

Hand Stack: Utilizing both hands to create a jam in a wide crack.

Headwall: A large expanse of overhanging rock.

Heel Cup: The heel of the shoe.

Heel Hook: Hanging by the heel.

Hueco: A shallow depression in the rock.

Imaging: Watching climbing and recording it in your mind sub-consciously.

In-cut: A hold you can get your fingers behind.

Jam: Expanding a part of your body to hold it in place in a crack.

Knee-back: Opposition utilizing the knees against one wall and the back against the other wall.

Knob: A protrusion from the rock.

Lateral Stiffness: The quality of a climbing shoe that prevents it from moving from side to side.

Layback: Pulling with the hands and pushing with the feet.

Leader: In a roped safety system, the leader climbs first and places protection.

Leavittation: A method of climbing wide cracks utilizing knee locks and hand stacks.

Lip: The edge of an overhang.

Lunge: Jumping for a hold.

Mantle: Boosting yourself on a hold or ledge by locking the elbows and bringing the feet up.

Match Hands, Match Feet: Placing both feet or both hands on the same hold.

Mountaineering: Climbing involving snow or ice.

On-sight Ascent: Climbing a route for the first time without falling, without any prior knowledge about the climb.

Off-hands, Off-fingers Jams: A jam slightly larger than a hand jam or a finger jam.

Off-width: A crack that you can get your arms and legs in, but not your entire body.

Open Grip: Palm open, finger tips resting on the hold.

Opposition: Pushing in two different directions.

Outside Corner: Where two planes of rock meet to form a vertical arete.

Overhang: A portion of rock that exceeds 90 degrees.

Palming: Placing the entire hand over a rounded hold.

Pinch Grip: Pinching the sides of a hold.

Pinnacle: A solitary shaft of rock that is separated from or leans against other rocks.

Piton: A type of protection that is hammered into cracks. Rarely used in modern free climbing.

Pockets: Small holes in the rock formed by trapped gas or solution.

Polish: Slippery rock formed by abrasion from water or glaciers.

Positive Pull: A handhold that you can pull downward on.

Protection: Devices placed in the rock to catch a falling climber.

Push-off: Pushing upward off of a positive hold.

Rand: The rubber side of a climbing shoe close to the sole.

Ratings: Degrees of difficulty for climbs.

Redpoint: The ascent of a climb without a fall after many attempts.

Ring Grip: Using the thumb to hold down a finger.

Roof: See Ceiling.

Second Class Climbing: Hiking up steep and uneven terrain.

Sequence: Certain movements that are needed to climb a climb.

Side-pull: A hold that is grasped sideways.

Sixth Class Climbing: See Aid Climbing.

Slab: See Apron.

Smearing: Pressing as much rubber as you can into the rock to take advantage of the most friction.

Static Climbing: Climbing in control with no jumping or sudden movements.

Stem: Pressing both feet against opposite holds.

Tape: Adhesive cloth tape used to protect the hands when climbing cracks.

Thank God Hold: See Bucket.

Tips: A crack that is too small to stick your fingers in.

Toe cam: Wedging your toe against your heel.

Toe Jam: Twisting your toe in a crack.

Toeing in: Pressing the toe of the boot into a crack that is too thin to toe jam.

Top Rope: A roped safety system whereby a rope is dropped from the top of a cliff.

Torque: Twisting motion of a cam.

Traverse: Sideways climbing movement.

Vertical Grip: Pressing the tips of the fingers into a hold with the first digits bent outward and the other digits bent inward.

Visualization: Rehearsing a movement in your mind before doing it.

INDEX

Abrasion & Impact: 52
Aid Climbing: 4-5, 59
Anchor: iv, 59
Apron: 59
Arete: 38, 59
Balance: 12, 59
Barndoor: 23, 59
Belay, Belayer: 23, 59
Beta: 59
Bouldering: 51, 55, 59
Bucket: 59
Bulge: 38, 59
Buttress: 36, 59
Cam: 48, 59
Case-harding: 40, 59
Chalk: 11, 59
Chickenhead: 40, 59
Chimney: 38, 59
Ceiling: 38, 59
Climbing Gyms: 55, 59
Cling Grip: 22, 59
Combinations: 31, 59
Competitions: 58, 59
Corner: 38, 59
Crab Crawl: 59
Crack & Face Combinations: 49
Cracks: 38, 41
Cross-hands, Cross-feet,
   cross-over, cross-through: 60
Deadpoint: 35, 60
Dihedral: 38, 60
Dike: 40, 60
Dome: 60
Down Climbing: 17
Dynamic Climbing: 27, 60
Edge, Edging, Edging Boot: 18, 60
Exfoliation: 36, 38, 60
Exposure: 60
Finger Crack, Finger Lock: 38, 43, 60
Finger Jams: 43
Fifth Class Climbing: 5-8, 60
First Aid: 53
First Class Climbing: 5, 60
Fist Crack, Fist Jam: 38, 44, 60
Flake: 38, 60
Flash Ascent: 7, 60
Follower: 60
Fourth Class Climbing: 5, 60
Free Climbing: 4, 60
Free Soloing: 5, 60

Friction: 12, 60
Friction Hold, Friction Boot: 20, 60
Hand Crack, Hand Jam: 38, 41-42, 60
Hand Stack: 48, 61
Headwall: 38, 61
Heel Cup: 61
Heel Hook: 32, 61
Hueco: 39, 61
Imaging: 55, 61
In-cut: 61
Intrusions: 40
Jam: 41, 61
Knee-back: 28, 61
Knob: 40, 61
Large Formations: 36
Lateral Stiffness: 61
Layback: 30, 52, 61
Leader: 61
Leavittation: 48, 61
Lip: 35, 61
Lunge: 27, 61
Mantle: 26, 61
Match Hands, Match Feet: 61
Mountaineering: 61
Movement: 15
Objective Dangers: 52
On-sight Ascent: 7, 61
Off-belay: 57
Off-hands, Off-fingers Jams: 38, 44, 61
Off-width: 38, 45, 61
Open Grip: 21, 61
Opposition: 23, 25, 28-31, 61
Outside Corner: 38, 62
Overhang: 32-35, 62
Palming: 25, 62
Pinch Grip: 23, 62
Pinnacle: 36, 62
Piton: 62
Pockets: 24, 62
Pocket Pulls: 52
Polish: 40, 62
Positive Pull: 21-22, 62
Protection: 62
Push-off: 26-27, 62
Rand: 62
Ratings: 5-7, 62
Redpoint: 7, 62
Ring Grip: 62
Root: 38, 62

Safety: 50-53
Second Class Climbing: 5, 62
Sequence: 62
Shoes: 9-11
Side Pull: 23, 62
Sixth Class Climbing: 5, 62
Slab: 62
Small Formations: 39
Smearing: 62
Static Climbing: 62
Stem: 28, 31, 62
Stretching & Conditioning: 51
Tape: 49, 62
Tendonitis: 51-52
Thank-God Hold: 35, 62
Thin Cracks: 43
Thin Face Climbing: 52
Third Class Climbing: 5
Tips: 63
Toe Cam: 63
Toe Jam: 43, 63
Toe Locks: 32
Toeing in: 43, 63
Toe Rope: 54, 63
Torque: 63
Traverse: 15-17, 63
Undercling: 31
Varnish: 41
Vertical Grip: 22, 63
Visualization: 32, 55, 63

Explore the Outdoors

Each only $4.95

The Basic Essentials Series

Backpacking
Harry Roberts
ISBN 0-934802-44-0

**First Aid For
The Outdoors**
Dr. William Forgey
ISBN 0-934802-43-2

Map & Compass
Cliff Jacobson
ISBN 0-934802-42-4

**Edible Wild
Plants and
Useful Herbs**
Jim Meuninch
ISBN 0-934802-41-6

Canoeing
Cliff Jacobson
ISBN 0-934802-39-4

Camping
Cliff Jacobson
ISBN 0-934802-38-6

ICS BOOKS, Inc.

Ask for any of these titles at your favorite outdoor equipment outlet or bookstore.
For a coplete catalog of ICS Book titles for outdoor lifestyles call 1-800-541-7323.